A Wacky Guide to Food Fun

ALAN SNOW

Dear Food Funatic

We all know that food is what you eat. What most people don't know is that there are many other useful, extraordinary and entertaining things that you can do with it. In this book I've cooked up a hotpot of ideas to whet your appetite, but before you start you'll need to remember these 5 important rules.

1. If you are going to make a mess, make sure you cover your work surface, wear your oldest clothes and tidy up afterwards.

2. Read the list of things you need before you start and make sure you have everything.

3. When you see this sign, ask a grown-up to help you.

4. NEVER waste food. Measure it very carefully. Don't use more than you need.

5. **KITCHEN SAFETY CODE:**
   - Wash your hands before you make anything to eat.
   - Don't leave saucepan handles pointing out.
   - Wear oven gloves when you touch anything hot.
   - Wash things up as you go along.
   - Be very careful when you use knives.

Contents

How to Make an Empty Egg

You need a clean egg, a large needle, a small bowl and an eggcup.

1. Use the needle to make a tiny hole in the pointed end of the egg.

2. Make a bigger hole (about 3 mm across) in the rounded end.

3. Hold the egg over the bowl and blow as hard as you can through the small hole. Keep on blowing until all the white and yolk has come out. The egg will now feel very light.

(Keep the yolk and white in the fridge. It can be used in cooking.)

4. Wash the empty egg and put it in an eggcup, large hole down, to drain and dry.

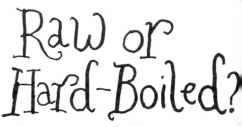

Eggsac Things With

Raw or Hard-Boiled?

Say to a friend, "Bet you can't tell which of these eggs is raw and which is hard-boiled without opening them!"

HOW TO DO IT

1. Turn the plate upside down and put it on a flat surface.

2. Carefully hold one of the eggs, pointed end down, between your thumb and forefinger and try to spin it on the plate. If it is hard-boiled, it will spin. If it is raw, it will fall over.

? ?

You need a raw egg,
a hard-boiled egg
and a plate.

Tyrannosaurus Reggs

You need an empty egg, a small saucepan, green food colour, 2 squares of lime jelly, water, Blu-Tack, a small plate, a sheet of paper and an eggcup.

1. Put the empty egg in a saucepan with some cold water and a few drops of green food colour. Boil the empty egg for 10 minutes. Let the water cool down and then take the green egg out of the saucepan.

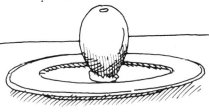

2. Make the jelly according to the instructions on the packet. Let it cool down but don't let it set.

3. Stand the empty egg, pointed end down, on a piece of Blu-Tack on the plate.

4. Roll up the sheet of paper to make a funnel.

5. Put the sharp end of the funnel into the hole in the rounded end of the egg, and then carefully pour in the cool liquid jelly until the egg is full.

6. Put the the egg on its plate in the fridge and leave it there for a few hours to set.

7. When you are ready to eat your tyrannosaurus regg, either put it in an egg-cup and eat it like a boiled egg, or peel it VERY carefully like a hard-boiled egg.

The Jet-Powered Soda Squirter

You need some baking powder, sticky tape, a plastic bottle, water, a drinking straw, Plasticine, clingfilm, 2 tissues and cotton.

1. Put 3 teaspoons of baking powder in a tissue and tie it around with a piece of cotton, leaving a long end free.

2. Half fill the bottle with water. Stick your finger inside a tissue and use it to dry around the inside of the bottle neck.

3. Push the packet of baking powder into the neck and leave it hanging by taping the cotton to the outside of the neck. DO NOT LET THE POWDER GET WET!

4. Slide the straw into the bottle. Push Plasticine around it to block up the neck.

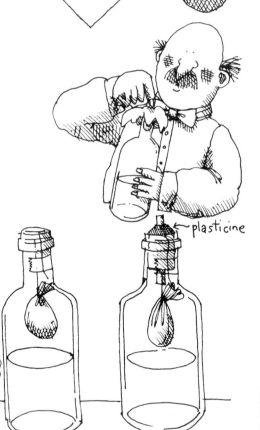

—plasticine

5. Wrap the neck in clingfilm to keep it waterproof.

6. Shake and squirt!

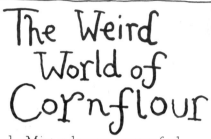

The Weird World of Cornflour

1. Mix a large spoonful of cornflour with water until it forms a thick creamy gunge!

Stir it slowly... it feels like a liquid!

Stir it hard and quickly... it feels solid!

...hen...ce First Helping

You need a packet of cornflour, water, a spoon and a mug.

2. Now experiment with this strange stuff.

Try pulling the spoon out very quickly.

Hit the surface with a spoon - see if you can make it crack!

The Astounding Gravity-defying Liquid

You need a large wide glass, half a scooped-out orange, vegetable oil, water, a drinking straw and scissors.

1. Scoop out the inside of the orange half, making the surface as smooth as possible.

2. Poke 2 small holes in the bottom of the upturned half with the scissors.

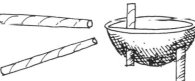

3. Cut 2 short pieces off the straw and stick them into the holes so that one sticks up and the other down.

4. Squeeze the upturned orange into the glass about halfway down.

5. Pour the oil into the glass so that it trickles through a straw to the bottom. Stop when the oil reaches the base of the orange.

6. Now pour the water slowly into the glass until it nearly reaches the rim. Watch. Small globes of water will slowly sink to the bottom of the glass, and the 2 liquids will gradually swap places!

← oil
← water
water globes → sink
← oil

Frankenstein's Face Cake

You need 2 300 g swiss rolls, 100 g of strawberry jam, 4 liquorice spirals, 8 cocktail sticks, a spoon, a knife and a plate.

1. Daub a circle of jam on the middle of the plate.

2. Cut a thick slice from one of the swiss rolls and stick it on the jam. Cover this with jam. Stand the rest of the roll on top.

3. Cut 2 slices from the other roll. Halve one and cut a quarter off the other.

4. Use the halves for ears and the quarter for a nose. Stick them on with jam, and support them with a cocktail stick each.

5. Take the liquorice sweets from the middle of the spirals. Spike each with half a cocktail stick and fix them on as eyes and as bolts through the neck.

6. Cut the liquorice spirals into strips and hang them down, like hair.

7. If you've got a strip left over, pin it on as eyebrows, using another cocktail stick cut in half.

8. Remember to remove the cocktail sticks before you eat the cake!

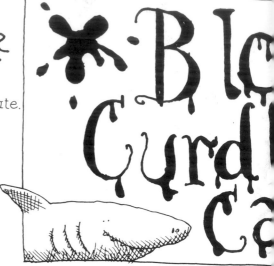

Shark-infested Cheesecake

You need a packet cheesecake, blue food colour, some thin, square after-dinner mints, a knife and a small lump of marzipan.

1. Make up the cheesecake, following the instructions on the packet. But...add 6 drops of blue food colour to the topping as you stir it!

2. As soon as you've poured the topping onto the cake, carefully cut out shark-fin shapes from the mints.

3. Push the fins into the blue topping in a circle formation. Use the knife to create ripples in the water behind each fin!

4. Make a raft by placing a mint flat in the middle of the fin circle.

5. Mould the marzipan into a small sailor shape. Give him a sailor's hat by cutting a small triangle of mint and sticking it upright on his head! Stand him on the raft and leave him to his fate! (If he falls over, make him sit.)

Vegosaurs

You need some potatoes (the weirder the shape the better!), carrots, cloves, used matchsticks, a knife and a chopping board.

1. Use a potato for the vegosaur's body. (Half potatoes make good tortoise shell shapes.)

2. Cut carrots to make legs, a neck and a tail. Join them to the body using the matchsticks as joints.

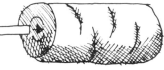

3. To make a large head, cut a carrot like this and twist the neck round.

neck

head

4. Slice carrots down the middle for the feet to help balance the vegosaur.

5. Cloves make good eyes and spikes.

6. Matchsticks can be used for fangs, arms and spikes. Cut a slice out of the head to make an open mouth.

Priceless Popcorn

1. Paint the popcorn in different colours. When dry varnish each piece and leave overnight.

Things With Food

You need some ready-made popcorn, poster paints, a paintbrush, varnish, a needle and some cotton.

2. Thread the popcorn onto the cotton to make necklaces and bracelets.

Kitchen Clay Modelling

You need 40 g of baking powder, 20 g of cornflour, a tablespoon of water, a spoon, a saucepan, clingfilm and a rolling-pin.

1. Mix the baking powder and cornflour together in the saucepan. Add the water and stir into a stiff paste. (Add a little more water if it's too dry.)

2. Heat briefly at a low heat, stirring till you see the mixture beginning to expand. Take it off the heat and leave it to cool in the fridge under some clingfilm for 10 mins.

3. Take the mixture out, knead it gently and roll it out like pastry. Now model it into whatever shape you like – but HURRY! It dries out quickly.

4 Leave your shapes to dry in a warm place. Then paint and varnish them.

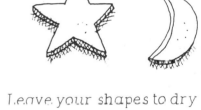

SOME IDEAS

Shark's-tooth necklace: Make lots of tooth shapes and poke holes through the sides with a bent paperclip. When dry, paint and varnish them and thread them onto some cotton.

Dice: Shape the mixture into a cube. Carefully press a bent paperclip into each side to make the dots.

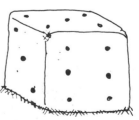

Space Survivor Kit

(Perfect for transporting your cocktails on dangerous missions!)

You need a drink, 2 small plastic bags, a drinking straw, 2 rubber bands (1 small, 1 large) and some sticky tape.

1. Pour your drink into one of the plastic bags.

2. Stick in a straw.

3. Seal it up tight with tape.

4. Seal the straw by bending it in half and putting a small rubber band over it.

5. Seal all this up in the second "safety" bag, tying it with the other rubber band.

6. When you're thirsty, release the straw and drink!

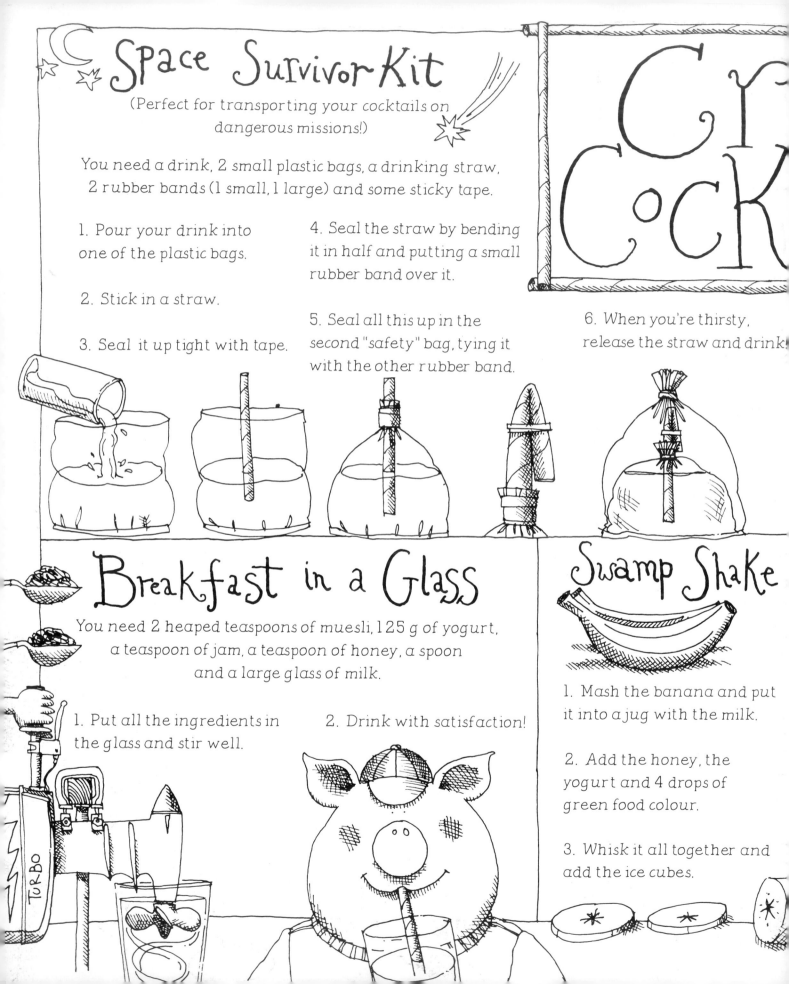

Breakfast in a Glass

You need 2 heaped teaspoons of muesli, 125 g of yogurt, a teaspoon of jam, a teaspoon of honey, a spoon and a large glass of milk.

1. Put all the ingredients in the glass and stir well.

2. Drink with satisfaction!

Swamp Shake

1. Mash the banana and put it into a jug with the milk.

2. Add the honey, the yogurt and 4 drops of green food colour.

3. Whisk it all together and add the ice cubes.

azy tails

Wobbly Sunrise

You need 6 cubes of red jelly, Ribena, 1 pint of orange juice, 4 straws, 4 tall glasses and a Space Survivor.

1. Make the jelly by adding half of a pint of hot water to it, stirring and adding enough water to make it up to a pint. Wait for it to cool before pouring 4 or 5 cm in the bottom of each glass.

2. When the jelly is set, pour the orange juice on top.

3. Put some undiluted Ribena in the Space Survivor. Poke its straw into the orange so it's just above the jelly and squeeze a little Ribena out.

4. Admire the sunrise, then stick your straw into your jelly and SUCK!

You need a banana, 2 teaspoons of honey, 125 g of yogurt, green food colour, 4 ice cubes, a pint of milk, a jug and a whisk.

13

Hand Sandwich

You need 3 frankfurter sausages, some tomato ketchup, butter or margarine, 2 slices of bread, 5 pieces of sliced almond, a knife and a plate.

1. Cut the sausages in half lengthways (eat one of the halves now - you only need 5).

2. Poke an almond slice into one end of each of the 5 sausage halves to make fingernails.

3. Butter both slices of bread and put one slice on a plate.

4. Arrange the 5 sausage halves on the slice of bread to look like 4 fingers and a thumb.

5. Add lots of tomato ketchup.

6. Put the other slice of bread on top to make a sandwich.

7. Now offer the hand sandwich to a friend!

Bats and Bones Bolognese

For 2 hungry vampires

You need 2 392 g tins of bolognese sauce, 2 green and 2 white lasagne strips, 2 teaspoons of vegetable oil, scissors, a large saucepan of water and 2 plates.

1. Bring the pan of water to the boil. Add the lasagne strips and a teaspoon of oil. Boil them for about 10 minutes or until the strips are soft.

2. Drain the pan. Leave the strips on a plate to cool. Dab them with a little oil to stop them sticking.

3. Using the outlines as a guide, cut out bat shapes from the green strips and bones from the white.

4. Wash the saucepan! Open the tins of bolognese sauce and empty them into the pan. Add the shapes and mix in.

5. Heat the mixture, stirring well. When cooked, pour it onto your plates and sink your fangs in!

bat

bone

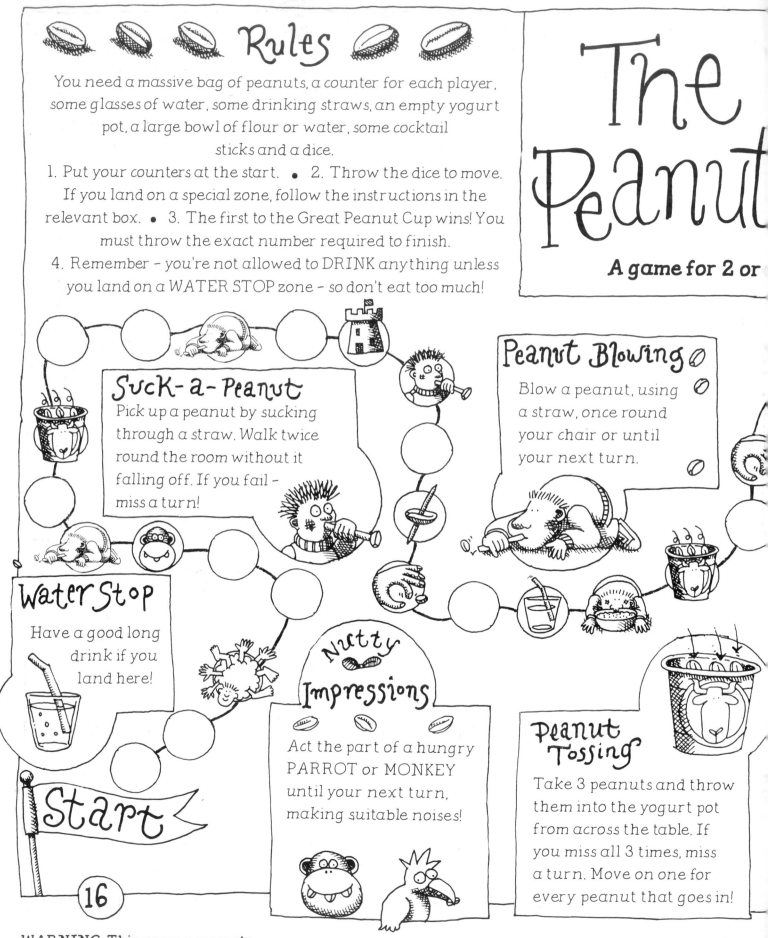

Rules

You need a massive bag of peanuts, a counter for each player, some glasses of water, some drinking straws, an empty yogurt pot, a large bowl of flour or water, some cocktail sticks and a dice.

1. Put your counters at the start. • 2. Throw the dice to move. If you land on a special zone, follow the instructions in the relevant box. • 3. The first to the Great Peanut Cup wins! You must throw the exact number required to finish.

4. Remember - you're not allowed to DRINK anything unless you land on a WATER STOP zone - so don't eat too much!

The Peanut

A game for 2 or

Suck-a-Peanut
Pick up a peanut by sucking through a straw. Walk twice round the room without it falling off. If you fail - miss a turn!

Peanut Blowing
Blow a peanut, using a straw, once round your chair or until your next turn.

Water Stop
Have a good long drink if you land here!

Nutty Impressions
Act the part of a hungry PARROT or MONKEY until your next turn, making suitable noises!

Peanut Tossing
Take 3 peanuts and throw them into the yogurt pot from across the table. If you miss all 3 times, miss a turn. Move on one for every peanut that goes in!

Start

16

WARNING: This game uses nuts.

Great Game

re players

Tower-Building Challenge

Challenge another player to build towers of half peanuts, one on top of the other. The highest tower after 30 seconds wins and the builder has another turn. The loser must go back 6!

Flick-a-Nut Challenge

Everyone picks a nut. Line them up on the table. Flick them as far as you can. The winner has an extra turn.

Bob-a-Peanut

Drop a peanut into the bowl of flour or water. Now try and get it out using your mouth only!

Bundle

Everyone gets up. Someone throws a peanut into the far corner of the room. On the word "go", everyone races to get the peanut, using EVERY means possible to win! The winner has another turn!

Cocktail-Stick Challenge

Everyone takes a small cocktail stick and a pile of peanuts. You've got 30 seconds to eat as many as you can, using the stick only. The winner has an extra turn!

The Pass the Pong Game

(Not good for people with colds!)

You need tissues, sticky tape, lots of smelly food (like cheese, herbs, spices, lemon peel, peppermints, garlic etc.), pens, paper and some willing sniffers!

1. Secretly gather 10 small samples of smelly foods from the kitchen. (Dry things are best - they're less messy!)

2. Wrap them separately inside tissues and seal them with tape. Number each packet.

3. Hold a competition for your friends. Give everyone a pencil and paper. Get them to write down the numbers 1 - 10.

4. Pass the packets around. They must smell each packet and write down what they think is inside.

5. Open the packets and find out who scored highest!

Fondle and Flinch!

You need some fondle-and-flinchers, 10 bowls, 10 foods with strange and nasty textures (like cold spaghetti, pork crackling, baked beans, mashed banana!), kitchen paper, a blindfold and a pen and paper.

1. Secretly place a different food in each bowl and cover with kitchen paper.

2. Bring the first victim into the room and blindfold him

Guessing

Yummy or Yuk!

(A tasty teaser!)

You need some tasters, a spoon and a blindfold each, plates, paper, a pencil, a chocolate bar, an onion and any other food you can cut up.

1. Secretly cut all the food into similar-sized pieces and put it on numbered plates.

2. Blindfold your friends and get them to hold their noses.

3. Spoon-feed a piece of each food to your friends in turn! They must whisper what they think the food is. Write down their answers.

4. When everyone has tasted everything, take the blindfolds off and reveal the answers. The winner is the taster with the most correct guesses!

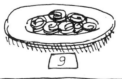

```
  1        2
  3        4
  5        6
  7    8    9
```

3. Uncover each bowl and let him touch each food in turn (wiping his hands clean between bowls!). Write down what he thinks each food is.

4. Take off his blindfold and let him watch while the other players have their turns.

5. The winner is the player with most correct answers.

Winner

Fondant (ready-made) icing can be sculpted into anything and eaten on its own, but to make a horribly realistic fried-breakfast cake read on…

You need a sponge cake, 500 g of ready-to-roll icing, icing sugar, a clean paintbrush, red, yellow and blue food colour, some saucers, a glass of water and a rolling-pin.

1. Buy or make a large sponge cake without a topping. Cover the cake top with a layer of rolled-out icing. Dust it lightly with icing sugar.

2. Squish out some icing to make a flat fried-egg shape. Put it on the top of the cake. Add a round dome for the yolk.

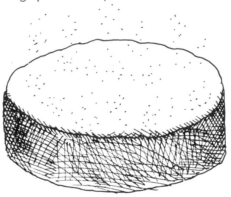

3. Make some bacon by rolling out a slightly thicker slab of icing, keeping it wide at one end and narrower at the other. Make a few bumps and ripples along the surface.

4. Make lots of little oval pellet-sized lumps for baked beans! Scatter them in a corner.

5. Make chips by cutting rectangles out of a thick, flat piece of icing.

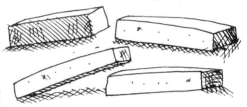

6. Make button mushrooms by pressing out a little fat cap with your thumb, then sticking a short rounded stalk inside.

7. Make a fried tomato from half a ball of icing, slightly squashed around the edge.

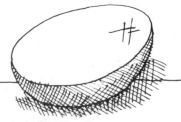

Fried-fast ~~Ze~~

9. When you've arranged your breakfast, drip a few drops of food colour on a saucer and experiment mixing them with the paintbrush. If you've got a small strip of icing left over you can use it to try out your colours.

10. A Short Colour Guide

red + yellow = orange
red + blue + yellow
= brown

More water = paler colour

Yolk: yellow + orange
Beans: orange (stain the
icing around the
beans orange to
make the sauce!)

Tomato: red + orange
Bacon meat: orange +
pale red
Bacon fat: yellow + brown
Chips: yellow
Mushrooms: pale brown,
Sausage: brown

11. Serve up your
astounding cake!

8. A cocktail sausage rolled in your fingers could complete the meal!

Balloonostatics (Part 1): Bendy Water

You need a balloon and a tap.

1. Blow up the balloon and rub it on your hair or woolly clothes to give it a charge.

2. Turn on the tap so that a gentle stream of water comes out.

3. Move the balloon slowly towards the stream. If the water doesn't bend, try rubbing the balloon again.

Balloonostatics (Part 2): Dancing Cornflakes

You need some cornflakes, a plate and a balloon.

1. Crush the cornflakes into small pieces and sprinkle them lightly on the plate.

2. Blow up a balloon and rub it against your hair or woolly clothes to build up an electric charge.

3. Hold the balloon low over the cornflakes and pass it slowly back and forth. If the cornflakes don't twitch and leap, rub the balloon and try again.

22

hen ice

Second Helping

Stripy Celery

You need a stick of celery, red or blue food colour and a cup of water.

1. Mix 4 or 5 drops of food colour with the water.

2. Cut the bottom off the celery and stick it into the water.

3. Wait overnight. In the morning the celery will be stripy. The celery's xylem – the tubes for sucking up water and food – are stained with food colour.

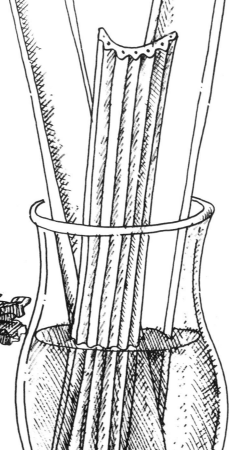

The Fantastic Radish Crane

You need a large fresh radish with its stalk still attached, a knife, a spoon, a plate and some thread.

1. Cut the radish in half.

2. Scoop out the middle of the top half, leaving a small crater. Be careful not to damage the edge.

3. Tie a piece of thread round the stalk.

4. Press the radish down gently on the middle of the plate. Lift slowly using the thread. The plate should be raised up by the power of suction.

The Pudding from Another Planet

You need a 250 g pack each of red, yellow and green jelly,
a 200 g tin of pineapple rings, a 425 g tin of custard,
10 grapes, a dinner plate, a pudding basin that will fit
when up-turned on the plate, a knife,
3 potatoes and 3 used matchsticks.

1. Make the red jelly according to the instructions. Fill the bottom third of the basin with the jelly and put it in the fridge.

2. When it is thick and almost set, arrange the pineapple rings in the jelly round the side of the basin. Let it set.

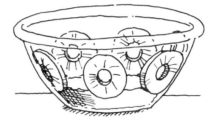

3. Make the green jelly and then pour enough on top of the red jelly to fill the middle third of the basin. Let it set.

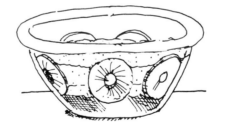

4. Make the yellow jelly and pour it on the top of the green jelly to fill the basin.

5. When the jelly has set, fill a washing-up bowl with warm water and stand the basin in it for a minute (don't let the jelly get wet).

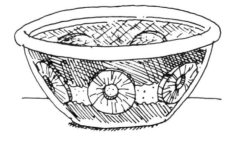

6. Take the basin out of the water and place the plate upside-down on top. Carefully turn them over and slowly lift the basin up off the jelly.

7. Spoon the custard round the jelly on the rim of the plate. Decorate with grapes.

24

...atic ...serts

Worm Pudding

You need 80 g of plain egg noodles, 2-3 300 g cans of chocolate rice pudding, 6 crushed biscuits, 60 g desiccated coconut, red and green food colour, spoons, a pan and small and large bowls.

1. Cook the noodles according to the instructions. Put 10 drops of red food colour in the water. Leave the noodles in the red water to cool. These are the worms!

2. Empty the rice pudding into the large bowl to make the soil and stir the crushed biscuits in, for stones.

3. Drain the worms and mix them into the soil. Pat the surface down.

8. Make legs for the spaceship by cutting each potato in half and fixing the halves on to the ends of the matchsticks.

9. Stand the 3 legs on a table and balance the jelly plate on top.

4. Put the coconut in the small bowl and add drops of green food colour. Mix it well until it is all green.

5. Sprinkle the coconut thickly and evenly on the soil to make a lawn.

6. If you like, you could make some fondant-icing flowers to grow on the grass.

25

Sox and Cress

You need an old sock, water, some cress seeds, paper and a large plate.

1. Soak the sock in the water till it's wet through. Put it on the plate and sprinkle the seeds onto it.

2. Cover them with pieces of paper to keep them damp and in the dark.

3. When the seeds begin to sprout, take the paper off and put the sock near a window. Keep it damp.

4. When the cress is 3 or 4 cm tall, pick and eat!

Recycled Vegetables

You need some vegetable-tops (such as carrot, parsnip, beetroot or onion), shallow dishes, pebbles and water.

1. Place a layer of pebbles in each dish and add enough water to cover them.

2. Place each vegetable-top in a dish.

3. Keep them well watered in a light place. New shoots should appear after a few days.

4. The onion leaves are good to chop up and eat in salads, but the other plants don't taste good at all!

hen ening

Pot an Avocado

You need an avocado stone, a flowerpot, potting compost, water, a rubber band and a polythene bag.

1. Fill the flowerpot with compost and water it.

2. Push the avocado stone into the compost with the blunt end pointing down. Cover it with a sprinkling of compost 1 cm deep.

3. Leave the pot in a warm, dark place, keeping the compost damp, until a shoot appears. It may take 2 or more weeks.

4. Put the polythene bag over the top of the pot and fasten it with the rubber band. Leave it in a warm and sunny place until the plant is a few centimetres tall, then take the bag off. Continue to keep the compost damp and feed your plant occasionally.

Pips and Seeds

You need some seeds or pips: orange, lemon or melon pips, pepper (capsicum) or tomato seeds, yogurt pots, potting compost, water, polythene bags and rubber bands.

1. Wash the seeds and dry them. Leave them for a day.

2. Plant them in the yogurt pots and label the pots. Follow the avocado instructions, stages 3-4.

Incredible Ices

You need lots of yogurt pots, spoons or lollipop sticks, and an assortment of drinks and delicacies (see below).

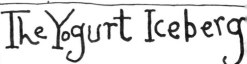

The Basic Method (A fruity Sucker)

1. Make sure the yogurt pot is clean.

2. Pour in some orange juice and add a few fizzy sweets.

3. Stick a spoon in at a slant and put the pot in the freezer.

4. When you want to eat the lollipop, dunk the yogurt pot in a bowl of hot water for a few moments.

5. Push in the bottom of the pot to force the Fruity Sucker out, grab the spoon…and get to work!

The Yogurt Iceberg

Ingredients: your favourite yogurt, nuts and chopped-up chocolate.

1. Take the lid off the yogurt.

2. Mix in the nuts and chocolate, add the spoon and freeze.

Other useful ingredients: fizzy drinks, milk, broken biscuits and Maltesers. Mix them and see!

The Jelly Licker

Ingredients: 3 jelly cubes and some Smarties.

1. Make up the jelly and pour it into the pot.

2. Add the spoon and some Smarties and leave it to freeze!

WARNING: This recipe contains nuts.

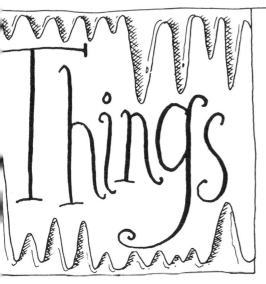

Things

Chocolate Rat Cake

You need a saucepan, a wooden spoon, a rolling-pin, a bowl, a chopping board, 75 g sugar, 75 g butter, 1 tablespoon of drinking chocolate, an egg, a packet of Rich Tea biscuits, a liquorice string, 3 chocolate peppermint sticks, a glacé cherry and 2 small pink sweets.

1. Wrap the biscuits in cling-film or place in a plastic bag and crush into small pieces using a rolling-pin.

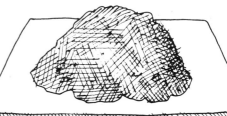

2. Using the wooden spoon, beat the egg in a bowl and then put it into a saucepan with the sugar, drinking chocolate and butter. Melt over a low heat and stir continuously until the mixture boils.

3. Remove the saucepan from the heat. Add the crushed biscuits to the mixture and leave it to one side for a few minutes to cool down.

4. Now place the mixture on a chopping board and mould into a rat shape. (Don't forget the ears.)

5. Add a liquorice tail, a glacé cherry nose, pink sweets for eyes and chocolate peppermint sticks broken in half for whiskers.

6. Put your rat in the fridge to get cold. Then eat him – quickly, before he escapes!

Flour · Painting

You need 50 g flour, 200 ml water, a saucepan, a spoon, a fork, some saucers, thick paper, cardboard, poster paints and a paintbrush.

1. Put the flour in a saucepan and gradually add the water until you have a smooth mixture.

2. Heat the mixture over a low heat. Keep stirring until it is thick and then remove the saucepan from the heat.

3. Wait until the mixture has cooled down and spoon it onto the saucers (one for each colour you want to use). Mix paint into the mixture. If it is very lumpy, put it through a sieve until it is smooth before you add the paint.

4. Put a spoonful of the mixture onto the paper and spread it out using a piece of cardboard. Add different-coloured mixture in the same way until your paper is covered.

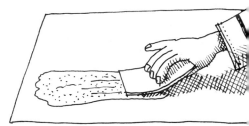

5. When you have finished, scrape pictures into the mixture using a fork, the end of a spoon or a piece of cardboard.

6. Let your flour-painting dry in a warm place.

Flat Fish

You need a mixing bowl, a wooden spoon, a fork, 150 g salt, 100 g plain flour, a dessertspoon of cooking oil, water, a baking tray, greaseproof paper, a fork, a paintbrush and poster paints or felt-tip pens.

1. Mix together the salt, flour and cooking oil, and gradually add enough water to make a lump of stretchy dough.

2. Roll ¾ of the dough into a ball. Flatten it onto a sheet of greaseproof paper on a baking tray until it is about 3 cm thick. Then shape it into the fish's body.

3. Use the remaining dough for your fish's tail, eye, lips and fins. You might want to add scales too. If the dough does not stick easily to the body, then brush it lightly with water. Try making patterns in the dough using a fork.

4. Put the baking tray in a cool oven for 2 to 3 hours. Remove when the dough has hardened.

5. Leave your fish to cool, then colour it brightly with paints or felt-tip pens.

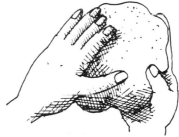

Goldfish Gobble

You need a carrot, a cheese-slice, scissors, a small glass pudding basin filled with water, and a friend.

1. Secretly, slice the carrot lengthways into long thin strips.

2. Cut the strips into fish shapes.

3. Drop the fish shapes into the basin of water.

4. Show your friend the bowl of goldfish. Now grab a goldfish and pull it, flapping, out of the water. Put it in your mouth, chew and swallow it!

First published 1993 by
Walker Books Ltd
87 Vauxhall Walk, London SE11 5HJ
This edition published 2007
2 4 6 8 10 9 7 5 3 1
©1993 Alan Snow
The right of Alan Snow to be identified as author of this
work has been asserted by him in accordance with the
Copyright, Designs and Patents Act 1988.
Printed in China   All rights reserved
British Library Cataloguing in Publication Data:
A catalogue record for this book is
available from the British Library
ISBN 978-1-4063-0636-1
www.walkerbooks.co.uk